The Life

of

Timothy Jones

Written by Tavetta Patterson

The Life of Timothy Jones

ISBN-10: 1539486605
ISBN-13: 978-1539486602

Dedication

I dedicate this book to:
My Mother, Brenda Jones
My Father, Warner Lewis III

My Grandparents:
Moses Jones Sr. and Sallie Jones
Warner Lewis Jr. and Mae Lewis
Evern Lewis

To my Brother Damien Lewis, thank you for inspiring me to do this book.

Mr. Jesse James Reed
December 1, 1945-October 24, 2016
Tim statement in memory of Mr. Jesse James Reed:
"He was a good man. Whatever I needed and whenever I needed him, he was there for me. He came to my basketball games. He built a ramp for me when I came home from the hospital so that I could get in and out of the house in the wheelchair. I knew him since I was in the fourth grade. He would take me on trips. He taught me a lot because I needed a positive male role model and he helped to lead me through various stages of my life. May he rest in peace."

Contents

Introduction

Written by Tavetta Patterson

Timothy Jones, affectionately known to many as "Tim" is very often the center of attention. A woman at a banquet that I attended with Tim asked, "Did you serve in the military or have you been in a war?" In a way, Tim was in a war. There is an undeclared street war that has ravaged lives, families, dreams and communities around the world. It is a war of senseless violence. You are reading "The Life of Timothy Jones" because he won the war by deciding to use his life for the good of humanity. Tim was shot in the head; however, he didn't allow that to stop his life. He still has love for humanity, faith in God, sincere joy, hope, goals and he still positively impacts people by sharing his story as he makes history.

When adults or children stare at Tim, he uses it as an opportunity to share his testimony. Tim usually begins the conversation like this, "Do you know what happened to me?"

The person will either say no or the person will try to guess what happened to Tim. When he tells the story about the day that he was shot in the head people are often amazed. When he informs them that the bullet is still in his head they are even more amazed and there is usually a look of shock.

His optimism, a tendency to look on the more favorable side of events or conditions, to expect the most favorable outcome, to believe that good ultimately predominates over evil in the world; is a part of what guides Tim each day. His faith in God is the foundation that gives him the strength to wake up each day in hopes of sharing his life story to help someone else on their journey through life.

After the dust settled and the newspaper headlines stopped being printed, this is the story of a family who had life as they planned it, interrupted by gun violence. Sound bytes are usually the method used to tell about the experience that Tim, his family, and millions of survivors around the world have endured. However, this book was written in their own words to amplify the voices of these courageous survivors.

"The Life of Timothy Jones" is a book about resilience in the midst of one of the hardest trials of life. This is the story of a young man who went through the process and did the work to live victoriously. This is the story of a family that chose love and joy. This book is a written testimony to remind you that tough times don't last, but tough people outlast tough times.

Tim is described by some people as

A Gentle Giant
A man full of grace
A man full of love
A mighty man of faith
A victorious man

Tim is my friend, an inspiration, a reminder of the faithfulness of God and a daily walking, talking miracle. I am honored that he chose me to share his story with the world. I hope that you are inspired to persevere after you read this book. I present to you, **"The Life of Timothy Jones."**

Chapter 1

Life in the words of Timothy Jones

I was a 15 year old, high school Junior, when I first began my high school football career. I started playing football at Horace Mann High School in Gary, Indiana. It was my God given talent because everyone thought I would be a star in basketball. I don't remember ever playing football as a child.

At the end of my high school experience I was great at playing three sports; baseball, basketball and football. I began as a defensive tackle during high school, playing football was as natural as breathing for me. People who watched me play said that I was a natural born football player. I believe that I inherited a gift because my father, Warner Lewis III and my uncle, James Jones were star football players at Horace Mann High School. My Father was named "Mr. Horace Mann" for the class of 1979 due to his athletics.

Playing football was an outlet for some of the anger I experienced as a teenage male growing up in Gary, Indiana. I led the state of Indiana in sacks during my senior year of high school.

I was labeled as being, "quick off the ball." As soon as they hiked the ball I was in the backfield. I weighed 310 pounds in my senior year of high school. I was like a machine that was equipped to run fast. My record was 4.5 in the 40 yard dash; which is considered fast for someone my size. After I ran it four times in a row, the coach added a position just for me. I was the fullback for our team.

The Mindset and Heart of a Champion

I was born with a winning mindset. When I was on the field I felt like I would win every game I played. I learned that you have to want it to win it. Two years of high school football led to the opportunity for me to play at the college level on a scholarship at Olivet Nazarene in Kankakee, Illinois. I learned about the college from Coach Brumm, my AAU Basketball Coach. He called me after reading about my football stats in the local newspaper.

I played basketball for the AAU Team under the leadership of Coach Brumm from 8th grade until 10th grade. During that time, I had the opportunity to play basketball against Corey Maggette and Quentin Richardson, they both made it to the NBA.

I also played basketball for Chase Elementary School and Horace Mann High School. Then Coach Brumm noticed that I was out growing basketball; however, he remained impressed by my ability to continue running on the basketball court. That year, I was told that Coach Piggee was the new football coach for Horace Mann High School. I told him that I played basketball and I was satisfied with basketball. Coach Piggee said, "If you don't play football then you won't play basketball anymore."

I decided to play football later that summer because I wanted to hold on to the opportunity to play basketball. After a year of managing basketball and football, I focused all of my attention football. I had an opportunity to visit Olivet Nazarene for a weekend during my senior year of high school. The experience allowed me to watch a college football game in a fun environment.

I decided to play football there because they were winning championships back to back and I have the mindset of a champion. In what would have been my second year attending college at Olivet Nazarene, the football team won a championship. During my official visit I also saw several beautiful girls and pre-planned the girls who were going to be my "study buddies."

I never had the opportunity to play football at a college level, but I spent nearly one year helping with the football team at Horace Mann High School after I graduated in 1997. From June 1997 until May 1998, I spent time lifting weights in the gym at the Hudson Campbell. However, the habit of drinking that I developed in high school as the result of negative peer pressure affected my life in a negative way.

The Turning Point: May 17, 1998

The day started with a visit to my house from the Assistant Coach of the Olivet Nazarene football team. I signed my letter of intent. After I signed my letter of intent, the Assistant Coach said, "Welcome to Olivet."

I was overjoyed so I called one of my friends to come to the house to try and get a scholarship to Olivet. I am the type of friend who wants the best in life for my friends. I was looking forward to going to college and carrying out my dreams on the football field.

I was scheduled to work that day. However, I decided to go celebrate my college acceptance with a group of friends from high school. One of my brothers worked for the same company, so he paged me and asked if I was coming to work that day. I called him back to share my good news. I told him that I wasn't going to work that day because I was going to celebrate at the beach. He asked me, "What are you celebrating?" I told him that I signed my college letter of intent.

After the phone call I went to the beach. About one hour after being at the beach we heard gunshots, so we all ran to the car. They said, "Is everybody alright? Is everybody alright? Is everybody alright?" After I heard the same question the third time I dropped my head.

I was told that they pushed me back to try to sit me up in the car and there was blood everywhere. They rushed me straight to the hospital. That is the last thing that I can remember. When I woke up in the hospital it was July 5, 1998. I had been in a coma for nearly two months of my life. There was also a trach tube inserted in my neck so I could not talk.

I had to write everything I wanted to know on a notepad. When I woke up from the coma, I asked my Mother why was she was crying. She said, "Doctor he is awake." Then she told me, "Tim you got shot in the head." As soon as she told me what happened, I felt pain in my head. I asked, "Why can't I move my body?" The doctor instructed me to be still. I asked, "Am I going home now?" They told me that I was in the hospital in Indianapolis, Indiana. I asked, "How did I get here?" They told me that the ambulance took me there while I was in a coma.

I began rehab and it was painful. The goal of the rehab team at the hospital was for me to learn how to walk again before being released to go home. There were many days that I cried during rehab because I was informed that the bullet was still in my head and if they removed the bullet they were concerned that I might die in the process.

The God Factor

God kept me in perfect peace throughout the whole experience in the hospital and rehab.

God continues to keep me in perfect peace on a daily basis. I made the commitment to God to spend the rest of my life dedicated to living for Him as a form of my gratitude. I am thankful that God saved my life.

September 12, 1998 was five days before my 19th birthday and the day I was scheduled to go home with my Mother. I had to be transported to outpatient Physical and Occupational Therapy. I had a nurse who came to the home while my Mother went to work. When she returned home from work she was my caregiver. I had to be transported by a wheelchair. I went through twelve years of outpatient rehab from 1998 until 2010.

By the grace of God, I learned how to talk again; walk again; how to move my arms and how to move my hands. My Grandmother on my mother's side of the family and my Great Aunts visited me when I was in the hospital. I drew strength from my Grandmother Sallie Jones; my Great Aunt Mozelle Williams and my Great Aunt Willie B. Odom.

A Life Forever Changed

What I miss the most is that I used to be out and about every day. I was popular when I was in school. Sometimes people tell me, they are angry that I can't protect them anymore. For some people, my large stature was very intimidating both on the streets and on the football field, but I am not that person anymore.

When I started going outside again after being shot in the head people would stare at me everywhere I went. I felt the same, because I am human. If they didn't know what happened to me all they had to do was ask me.

I never allowed anything or anyone to discourage me.

I am a strong man.

I am not afraid to tell people what happened to me.

I am proud of the fact that I survived what happened to me.

The experience just revealed how strong I am.

Although I don't know who shot me in the head I chose to forgive.

What are your favorite childhood memories?

Growing up I had a great family life. Everyone came to my Grandmother's house to enjoy the fun outdoor barbecue and family gatherings, which often fed many families in our neighborhood. My Grandfather, Moses Jones Sr. was a dedicated family man who wanted to take care of everyone; he was my first role model.

How did you get your memory back?

God did that! It is a blessing that God restored my memory, I can look at the words to the song for the praise team and most of the time it seems that I already know the song. For that and for so many reasons I say, "To God be all the glory."

I am proud of the life that I live. A lot of people thought I would be in the left field doing a lot of negative things with my life. However, I am in the right field living out the positive plans that God has for my life. It makes me feel good to know who I used to be compared to who I am now.

The old me, no matter where I went I would wear my hat to the left because gang banging was a part of my identity. I had gotten blessed into the vice lord gang at 11 years old in the 7th grade in middle school. A group of people surrounded me on the bus. I challenged them to fight me one on one, but they said, "No, you are too big." I did not want to join a gang, but I felt good, it gave me a lot of clout and a lot of people looked up to me.

Then when I would walk around the school with the other gang members everyone would be afraid of us in school. The rival gang was known as gangster disciples or folks. Once the folks who attended my middle school realized they could not beat us in fighting, they would call adult gang members to the school to fight us. Fighting became a way of life for me during my middle school and high school years. People would often pay me in high school to fight people for them. Or they would go to the liquor store and pay me with liquor. I did a lot in my life time that I was not proud of; however, I share my life story because there are a lot of young men dying in the streets. I often ask, "Why do so many young men have to die?"

What do you hope to leave as your legacy?

One hundred years from now I want people to know that I am a survivor despite all that I went through. I had the ability to go pro in football, but I let something negative get in the way of my success. However, I have learned that God wants me to speak to children, to encourage them to make right decisions, to keep them off the streets so that they can live to see their dreams come true. I love living and I hope to live to see 100 plus years of life, even with a bullet in my head. A lot of people think that there are just fragments of a bullet in my head; however, the whole bullet is still in my head.

I praise God that today I live free from the past. I walk with no gang pressure. I can walk into any neighborhood I choose without having to fight anyone. I know there are a lot of people who are still living a life of gang banging. I often ask them why, but for some people it is a way of life. Perhaps some people don't consider the fact that they have children who could get hurt in the crossfire or even worse they can be killed in the streets.

Progress from pain to purpose:

"I believe that I am worth saving, because God thought I was worth saving. Eyes haven't seen, ears haven't heard, all that God has in store for me. There is still so much more that is worth fighting for in my life." That is one of my favorite songs that I get to sing at church as part of the Praise Team. I love my church family. They mean so much to me. We laugh together and we accomplish so much together. On the mission team, different members of different groups discuss the lessons we have learned from the sermon taught by our Pastor. I am on the Mission Team with a group of Mothers who serve in the church. Today they gave me a gift bag full of goodies. I look forward to our meetings.

With the young people team we discuss peer pressure and ways to overcome peer pressure. We have plans to begin mentoring young people in the church so that they will have a way to talk through their struggles in life.

My goal is to help as many children as I can, so that they won't have to make the decision to exchange their dreams for life on the streets.

The one thing I enjoy most about being on the Praise Team is that I get the opportunity to sing praise to God on a regular basis. For a while I was the only male on the Praise Team, then another brother joined and we sing praises to God on a regular basis.

What challenges have you encountered since being home from the hospital?

One of the challenges was getting my feet to cooperate with my mind on a regular basis, because in my mind I walk really fast. My whole right side was weakened and I write with my right hand so I have to pause before writing. Sometimes that gets frustrating, but I know I have to move forward. I thought that would cause difficulty when I got ready to learn how to drive; however, I am determined to get my drivers license. I have never had my own license, so that is something I really look forward to in the near future. I have earned my permit and attended driving school. The instructor said a prayer with me, told me that he believed I could drive and we proceeded to take the driving test.

After the driving test he asked me, "Are you sure this is your first time driving a car?" I said, "Yes this is my first time driving a car." He said, "You did very good driving for the first time." That experience gave me a big boost of confidence. It made me feel proud of myself, especially after I said prayers the whole day until the driver picked me up from my house.

What are your plans for the future?

I am studying to obtain my drivers license so that I can drive myself and my family. I want this book to inspire people so that I can travel around the world to encourage people to stop the violence. I want to restore hope and I am on a mission to empower people to get anchored in the Lord because my soul has been anchored in the Lord. There was a time that I had a mouth full of curse words; however, since 2003 I have not used curse words; instead, I speak blessings and I sing for God.

When it is just me and God, I tell God that I want to travel all around the world telling my story because it is powerful and dynamic. I want to encourage children to be alert, because what happened to me could happen to them if they are not careful. I just knew I was going to the NFL after college. Being shot did not cross my mind, prior to the moment that it happened.

In fact, I did not know I had been shot until I woke up in the hospital. The night I got shot at the beach I was extremely drunk. However, I know that God had his hands over my life to protect me from the negative environment I was in and to protect me from death. I know some people who have died from being shot in the leg, so I truly understand how blessed I am to still be alive with the bullet in my head.

I had a conversation with God while I was in the hospital. I asked, "Why was I shot?" God answered, "You were moving too fast and needed to slow down." I told God, "If you let me live I will turn my life around and live for you." **"I am now living the plan of God for my life by travelling and speaking to inspire other people."**

Chapter 2

The Love of a Mother

September 17, 1979 at approximately 9:21p.m. a happy, healthy baby boy named Timothy Jones was born at Methodist Hospital Northlake in Gary, Indiana. He weighed 8 pounds and 7 ounces. He was the first of four sons born to Brenda Jones. He was the first grandchild born to Mr. Moses Jones Sr. and Mrs. Sallie Jones.

May 17, 1998 Timothy Jones returned to the same hospital where he was born. However, this time it was for a different reason.

The Life

of

Timothy Jones

In the words of his

Mother,

Brenda Jones

Brenda Jones is a Mother of four sons and four grandchildren who has exemplified the purest form of love. Their journey as a family had some bumps in the road. However, she was able to endure it all and help to nurse her son back to life.

How would you describe Tim as a child?

Tim was my daddy's favorite at that time. He was an eager, happy child. He attended Ambridge and Chase Elementary School.

How would you describe Tim as a teen?

Tim attended Tolleston Middle School then Horace Mann High School. He was nurtured in a close family. Tim was a good person who was very athletic. Tim was always outside; either, playing baseball or basketball. Therefore, it was a natural progression for him to attend college on an athletic scholarship. The atmosphere of the Jones household around graduation time was very excited. Tim was very happy that he had received a full scholarship for football. He was ready to go out and explore the world. I was happy for him because it was his dream to go to college and play football.

What were your dreams for Tim after high school?

I was happy for Tim. I was ready for him to go to college. I am glad he wanted to go to college, to see what college life was like. I wanted him to have the opportunity to explore the world and have a great experience. I really wanted him to be able to live his dream. I wanted him to be a nice young man out in the world like he was at home with me. I was eager for Tim to see what life would be like on his own, going to college, paying his own bills and living his dream. During that time, football was his dream, but perhaps now he has even bigger dreams!

How did you find out about the incident when Tim was shot in the head?

On the day that Tim was shot in the head I was in my room getting ready to go to bed. My son David knocked on the door and told me that Tim had been shot. I started breathing real hard, then I started telling myself to calm down, it is going to be alright. I did not really comprehend the depth of what happened so I went to the hospital alone. I thought maybe it was a graze, but it was more serious than that. I soon learned that I would need a support system to get through the journey.

When I arrived at the hospital I told them who I was and who I came to see. They told me to go in a room and have a seat. When I walked in the room I said, "Oh Lord, this is where the chaplain comes in and tell you the bad news." Then I said, "Don't think like that, think positive." The doctor came in the room and said that Tim had been shot in the head. They were cleaning him up, he was still responsive and very alert, but the way the bullet was lodged in his head they would not take a chance with moving the bullet. When they were done cleaning him then they would allow me into the room to see Tim. By that time my Mother, my sisters and my friend Gwen arrived at the hospital to be with me.

What happened when you first saw Tim after the shooting?

Tim looked like he had fallen and bumped his head. His head was wrapped in a bandage and he had to be put into a medically induced coma to be kept calm.

How did you endure all the days that Tim was in the hospital?

I was able to endure by praying. My support system was my entire family, the Zion Temple church family and my friend Gwen.

What happened during the recovery process?

Tim was cared for at Methodist Hospitals, St. Vincent Hospital in Indianapolis and Life Line was the therapy hospital. From June until September I travelled from Gary, Indiana to Indianapolis, Indiana for Tim to receive the medical treatment he needed. We did not have family in Indianapolis, Indiana so it was a hard experience, but I knew it was for the best.

Bringing Tim home:

When I was informed that Tim was coming home I was happy. I did not see it as a challenge. It was a new experience for me taking care of someone who could not walk, talk, feed himself or do for himself. I went to Indianapolis for two weeks to learn his medicines and how to dispense the medicines. I learned how to remove, clean and insert the trach tube. During the hospital stay Tim was also on a feeding tube so I learned how to feed him through a feeding tube. Then I learned how to properly lift Tim. It was a good experience. By the grace of God, when Tim was released from the hospital he made enough progress that he was able to have the feeding tube removed.

What challenges did you face on the journey to recovery?

I thought I would make a mistake, fall, lift Tim the wrong way or over medicate him. By the grace of God none of that became a reality and I was able to successfully care for Tim until he was nursed back to great health.

How did the Doctor explain what happened to Tim?

Dr. Anigbo at Methodist Hospital always called me Mom and he took the time to explain every step of the medical process. He showed me pictures of where the bullet was lodged in his brain and why they could not go in to move it. When we left Methodist to go to Indianapolis Dr. Anigbo said, "Be sure that Tim has a CT scan every year to be sure the bullet stays in place."

Every year for the past 18 years Tim had a CT scan and by the grace of God the bullet never moved. It is a miracle. God is a miracle worker. Tim has made significant progress. He went from being pushed in a wheelchair to walking on a cane. However, today he can walk on his own. I thank God, my family and the doctors who helped me with Tim. Wow, what an awesome job!

What would you say to a parent who may be currently experiencing what you experienced with Tim?

I would say, "It is going to be alright." When Tim was shot in the head, there was a lot of prayer, I believe in God, Tim believes in God and that is why Tim is still here. God had a plan for Tim and God still has a plan for Tim. God is not through with Tim yet. It is all about prayer.

Would you do anything different?

No. Tim had to learn how to walk, talk and feed himself. I was there to help him and we got through it together.

What are you most grateful for throughout the experience?

I am grateful that I knew how to take care of Tim. I am grateful for the friends and family who helped me care for Tim.

I am grateful for Lifeline in Indianapolis, because when I decided to go back to work they helped me find nurses in the Gary area for Tim.

There was a time that I thought I would not be able to return to work because Tim was not able to do anything for himself. Nevertheless, with their help I was able to return to work.

What are your hopes and dreams for Tim today?

I hope that he continues to trust in the Lord. Sometimes he appears to be afraid to learn how to drive, but I tell him to trust in the Lord and He will make a way. My dream for him is that he will still be able to live on his own. That is what he wanted to experience in college, to be a man who lives on his own. I believe he can drive and live on his own as an adult; he just has to put his mind to it.

Chapter 3

The Love of a Father

The Life

of

Timothy Jones

In the words of his Father,

Warner Lewis III

How did you find out about the incident when Tim was shot in the head?

I was incarcerated at the time. When I called home I was informed by telephone. I broke down and cried because Tim had just graduated from high school. When I saw Tim it was three years later in 2001. I visited Gary and Tim was in the process of learning to walk and talk.

How would you describe Tim as a teen?

I was incarcerated from 1996 until 2001 so I did not get a chance to see Tim play on the football field. However, Coach Piggee was also my Coach when I was in school so he told me about Tim and Jason and how great they were on the football field.

What are your hopes and dreams for Tim?

I have high hopes for Tim. I visit as often as I can. I always tell Tim, "I am just a telephone call away." I hope for the best for him. I love Tim and I love all my children.

Tim and his father ended their phone call with, "I Love You Man."

At the conclusion of the interview with Warner Lewis III, Tim shared reflections from high school:

I often asked Coach Piggee, "Am I better than my father on the football field?" Coach Piggee would tell me, "Boy you just don't know."

Chapter 4

Brotherly Love

Damien Lewis is very protective of his brother and wants only the best in life for Tim. During their childhood they shared time together at their grandparents' house on the weekends. Damien began playing football during elementary school; while Tim was playing baseball and basketball. However, by the time they reached high school they were brothers off the field and "football rivals" on the field. Damien played football for Roosevelt, while Tim and their younger brother, Jason played football for Horace Mann.

The Life

of

Timothy Jones

In the words of his

Brother,

Damien Lewis

How would you describe Tim as a child?

I didn't know anyone his age who knew sports as well as Tim and I didn't know anyone his age who could read as well as Tim. He would sit around and have discussions with our Grandparents. Tim was a smart bully, but it was not because he would take things from me; it was mainly because some people were intimidated by his presence. Tim was big and that was intimidating for some people.

What stood out about Tim as an Athlete?

Tim was so strong and fast for his size. It made him great in all three sports; football, baseball and basketball. To come from Horace Mann and get the recognition that he got made a huge difference. Tim could have gone to any college he wanted to attend. If Tim didn't get shot, I know he would have made it to the league. He was so strong he would have done well at the sport of his choice.

How did you find out about the incident when Tim was shot in the head?

We worked at an inventory company at the same time and we were scheduled to work that night. However, when I called Tim he told me that he was not going to work that day. I told Tim that I thought he was trippin' for missing work. Tim said, "I'm going to kick it, but I love you anyway."

I was going to go to the beach with a girl after work that night. However, when I got off work and called her, she said she had already been to the beach. She said we could not go back to the beach because there had been a shoot out at the beach. Shortly after that a cousin called me hollering and screaming on the telephone. She informed me that Tim had been shot in the head.

What have you learned from his life?

No matter what happens in life, you got to keep going. No matter what happens in life; whatever it is, it could be worst. For Tim to move around like he does with a bullet still in his head, I can't really complain.

The Life

of

Timothy Jones

In the words of his

Brother,

Jason Watson

Tim and Jason attended school together at Tolleston Junior High School and Horace Mann High School.

Tim graduated from Horace Mann in 1997 and Jason graduated from Horace Mann in 1998. They both played sports together and supported each other through various stages in life. Part of why they have achieved so much is because they've kept an eye on each other throughout the years.

How would you describe Tim as a child?

For me Tim was like a bully, but at the same time he was nice like a teddy bear. Sometimes he was mean and sometimes he was telling jokes. He would always find a way to cheer us up with jokes.

How would you describe Tim as a teen?

As a teen, that is when we became like best friends. Being around Tim I learned a lot from seeing how people loved him and how he made people laugh. I was shy as a child, but when I saw how outgoing Tim was that helped me to grow out of being shy.

How would you describe Tim as an adult?

His whole demeanor and attitude has changed. I can see the Lord all over him. I can see how God changed his life. Although he went through a tough situation he still has joy. Some people would be depressed, just based on the situation he went through, but Tim still chooses joy.

What age were you when you started playing football with Tim? What was it like playing on the field with your brother?

At around 15 we started playing football together at Horace Mann High School. Tim was the leader of the team and everyone looked up to him so I was happy to say that he was my brother. Tim looked out for me and protected me.

What stood out about Tim as an Athlete?

Tim was so much better than everyone on the field. No one could stop him. Tim was big and super fast as an athlete. Tim had a God given talent that you just can't teach a person.

How did you find out about the incident when Tim was shot in the head?

I was at home working on a project for school. I heard a banging on my door and it was one of our little brothers who came and told me what happened. Then I went straight to the hospital. I could not believe what happened to my brother until I made it to the hospital and saw all the blood and machines that he was hooked up to in the room.

What were your first thoughts?

I thought it was over for Tim, but God had other plans for him. What God has done for Tim is a miracle. A lot of people don't come back from that type of situation. For Tim to still be functioning and able to do all that he does in life is a miracle. I am so proud of Tim and all the work that he has done to get better and stronger every day. It is great to watch his progress in life.

What are your hopes and dreams for Tim today?

I hope that he keeps giving his testimony to encourage people. He loves to tell people how far God has brought him in life. I want Tim to succeed in everything that he does in life.

I want to see him receive all that God has for his life. I want him to be the best that he can be at whatever God has for him. I want to see him keep growing and striving to live the life that God has for him. In his mind, Tim still believes he is the same and you can't tell him different.

What have you learned from his life?

Don't ever give up, keep fighting, keep smiling and keep choosing joy. Even if you feel down or if you have tears rolling down your face at night, you wake up the next morning and keep smiling.

The Life

of

Timothy Jones

In the words of his

Brother,

Arthur London

Arthur London was involved with sports just like most of the men in his immediate family. His sports of choice were baseball and basketball. He also attended the family school, Horace Mann High School.

How would you describe Tim as a child?

Tim was the big brother that we all looked up to in life. Tim was always playing sports. Growing up we were all very close. We all played for the Brunswick Little League; David and I were in the Minor League and Tim was in the Major League.

How would you describe Tim as a teen?

I only saw Tim at home. He would always look out for us when he was at home. He was not at home that much because he was very often focused on sports.

How would you describe Tim as an adult?

Tim is an inspiration for a lot of people because of everything he has been through; sports are his passion, especially football. He helps with coaching football.

What stood out about Tim as an Athlete?

Tim was that guy who would surprise you. He was a lot
bigger than the other guys, but he could move just as fast or faster
than the other guys.

**How did you find out about the incident when Tim was shot in
the head?**

I was at home with my Mother.

What were your first thoughts?

I was just hoping that he was alright and that he was going
to pull through. Tim was loved by a lot of people and I didn't
know of him to have any enemies.

What are your hopes and dreams for Tim today?

I hope he continues to make a difference in the life of young men.

What have you learned from his life?

That anyone can do anything if they put their mind to it in life.

What do you hope to leave as your family legacy?

I hope people will know that we try to keep a positive image and set good examples.

What do you believe will help stop the violence?

When we were growing up we had a lot of opportunities and I believe that some of the violence would stop if children had more positive places to go, positive role models, and safe family environments to have fun.

The Life

of

Timothy Jones

In the words of his

Brother,

David O'neal

How would you describe Tim as a child?

I am the younger brother who always wanted to hang out with Tim, but he wouldn't let me roll with him until I was a teen.

How would you describe Tim as a teen?

It was a lot of fun because I was starting to hang around the people that Tim hung around, even the girls; they would like me as his little brother.

How would you describe Tim as an adult?

Tim has matured a lot since being shot in the head. He still likes to joke, but he is a lot more mature.

What school did you attend with Tim?

I attended Horace Mann High School with Tim and I graduated with the Class of 2000. I didn't play sports with Tim, but I always went to his games. All the coaches and people who watched him play were amazed because of his size and speed. He was a big dude who could run extremely fast. He was a good athlete at just about every sport he played.

How did you find out about the incident when Tim was shot in the head?

I was the first person called by telephone. I answered the telephone when the person who was with Tim called to inform my Mother that Tim had been shot. I was fixing a sandwich. He said, "Your brother got shot." I said, "Where did he get shot?" He said, "He got shot in the head." He sounded real sad when he told me so I thought Tim has passed away, but he didn't want to tell us by telephone. When he said it, I got sick to my stomach and threw my sandwich in the garbage.

Then I went to tell my Mother. I said, "Tim got shot." She was taking her time because Tim always ran the streets and I don't think she realized how serious it was until she got to the hospital. After that I didn't see my Mother for a long time because she was gone. She was going to different hospitals with Tim. I had to be responsible for taking care of myself. I didn't take it well because normally when people get shot in the head they don't make it.

When I went to school people were asking me what happened to my brother. They were asking me was my brother dead. There were people talking about my brother and saying he would be a vegetable. I didn't understand all that at the time. The next time I saw Tim after he got shot was when he moved back home. I didn't make it to the hospital to see him because he was transported to different hospitals out of the city. For me, it seemed like a whole year.

I went into his room and it was set up just like a hospital room. He still had tubes in his body when he came home. I said, "What's up Tim." Then he stretched out his hand and shook my hand. He was in his room a lot during that time. I don't really know how he got through that situation in his life. I do know Tim is a strong guy.

What are your hopes and dreams for Tim today?

I am glad that he did not pass away. I am glad that he got a second chance at life to do what he has to do for the rest of his life.

What have you learned from his life?

The lesson that I learned from his experience is to watch out for who you choose to hang out with in your neighborhood. It is important to watch your surroundings. It is important to try not to run the streets so much. I wish Tim didn't get shot. I wanted to see who he would have been as an athlete. So many people said he would have made it to the NFL when he was playing football in high school. Tim always told me that when he made it he was going to take me with him.

At the conclusion of our interview, David shared that he is 35 years young and currently on the waiting list for a kidney transplant. He recalled his first reaction, "When I first found out that I needed a kidney, I was feeling down about the situation, but I feel so much better now, I had to shake it off and I got my head up now." Perhaps David gains strength from thinking about the time he watched Tim recover at home.

The Life

of

Timothy Jones

In the words of his

Brother,

Jeremy Moore

How did you find out about the incident when Tim was shot in the head?

I lived in another state at the time so our Father told me about the incident.

What were your first thoughts?

I felt highly upset about the situation. I was distraught, but happy that Tim lived.

What are your hopes and dreams for Tim today?

I hope that he continues to grow. I want to see him complete his book and travel the world as a successful author.

What have you learned from his life?

His life changed all the way from what I heard about him before the incident.

What do you believe is the solution to stop the violence?

Everybody has tried different things, but I believe that it will take people getting together and communicating more.

What would you offer as hope to anyone going through a family tragedy?

Be sure to thank God that you are alive.

Chapter 5

Friendship through the growing pains of life

The Life

of

Timothy Jones

In the words of his Friend,

Shoneice Hicks

How did you meet Tim?

I met Timothy my sophomore year at Horace Mann High School while walking up the stairs to the 3rd floor. He was sitting on the floor on the radiator. He was looking at me so I hurried up and went to my locker. At some point he started calling me and we would talk on the telephone. They called him Debo and I called him Timothy. He would walk me home after school and it was the longest walk ever because everyone knew him. Even at that time I knew he was special, but I didn't realize how much until after the incident.

How would you describe Tim?

He is gentle, kind, patient, loving and laid back. Now he is funnier, he shares more jokes, he is more amazing and that is what made it easy for me to be friends with him.

What stood out about Tim as an Athlete?

He reminded me of Refrigerator Perry who played for the Chicago Bears. I would smile watching him. He had a confidence that said, "I bet you won't mess with me."

How did you find out about the incident when Tim was shot in the head?

When it happened I received a phone call from someone who was at the hospital. He said I needed to get to the hospital. I had never met Timothy's Mother. When they let me go see him in the hospital room, I remember holding his hand and I cried.

I was the last one in the room, when his Mother was being asked questions by the doctor. I knew that the doctor needed to know the truth about Tim because they were on a mission to save his life. It was a difficult conversation because his Mother was still in the hospital room. However, I had to share the real truth. Yes, Tim did smoke weed and yes he did drink. Yes he had tattoos, more than one to be exact.

During our interview for this book, his Mother, Brenda said, "I had never seen Tim drunk. It appears that out of respect for me, he was never in that condition when he was with me, so I appreciate that."

At the conclusion of the interview with Brenda Jones Tim reflected on the journey they have shared:

"I love her, she was there by my side, I am glad she helped me get my walking and talking back together. I apologize for anything I have ever done wrong."

What was it like to witness Tim go through the recovery process?

I was volunteering at the hospital during that time. I was also helping my grandparents and going to church, as a result I would visit Timothy every day. I told his Mother that I would sit at the hospital with him so she could go to work. When he went to the rehabilitation facility I went with his Mother. I learned CPR, learned how to feed him and how to clean the trach tube.

How were you able to endure the experience?

I know that it is in my heart to love people and to want them to do better. He is my friend and I wanted that for him. I thank God for putting love in my heart to take care of Timothy. I am glad that I was able to be there for him.

What are your hopes and dreams for Tim today?

He has a greater purpose. There is so much that Timothy has to offer. I speak life to him and I want to see him expand in the purpose that God has for his life. Timothy is different from the person I met on the 3rd floor of Horace Mann High School. He went from needing help to get into the house, to walking on a cane, to not needing any help to get into the house. I am so excited because someone needs to hear his story.

What have you learned from his life?

I learned to not take life for granted; to enjoy life; to not stress the small things in life. Timothy does not drive right now or have a car, but he gets to where he wants to go. In life there are choices, he chooses to wake up and keep going each day. Timothy inspires me to wake up each day, thankful for being alive.

Chapter 6

A Life of Faith

The Life

of

Timothy Jones

In the words of

Pastor Michael Dotson

He is the Pastor of Washington Street Church of God in Gary, Indiana. Tim calls him Pastor Mike and they share a close bond that has helped Tim in his walk with God.

When did you meet Tim?

I met Tim in 2003 at a house worship service. One of the neighbors on the next block from Tim attended the service and we have been hanging out ever since that day.

How would you describe Tim?

Tim is indomitable. He has the ability to keep going, he is a joy to be around, he is real personable and people are very fond of him.

What is his greatest accomplishment in ministry?

Tim is loyal. His loyalty and worship on the praise team. He is a great worshipper.

How did you find out about the incident when Tim was shot in the head?

Tim told me about the experience. It is by the grace of God that Tim survived. God intervened in something that could have been a tragedy and made something inspirational out of the experience. I had not met anyone like Tim, who had been shot in the head and survived to tell the story.

What do you believe will stop the violence?

I believe it will require an intervention of God and a revival amongst the churches. I meet young men like Tim quite a bit. I have a bunch of young men in my church or around my church who I am really concerned about. I am very concerned about the young men today. I seek opportunities to put more people in their path who are their contemporaries; people who may have come out of the streets, so that children can hear from someone they can relate to in life. I hope to help as many children as I can.

The issue of fatherlessness is the beginning of the path to despair and hopelessness, it is quite sad that some young men don't have anyone to man up with them when they need it most. A young man needs a man to show him how to be a man.

What is one of your greatest strengths?

Sometimes I forget, so it causes me to treat people the same. I don't look at people or life with disdain because I understand that I can learn a lot from people and people don't have to worry about me belittling them or thinking I am on a higher level of life than they are in life.

What was a significant turning point in your life?

I grew up in Gary, Indiana. A woman at my high school asked me did I want to go to college, despite the fact that I was the last one she should have considered. I left Gary, Indiana and went to college at Purdue University in West Lafayette. I believe that helped to save my life.

I did not plan to come back; however, when I was in my twenties, I had failed out of school, I had a terrible night and decided I needed help. I gave my life to Christ. Then God rebuilt my life, allowed me to go back to college and I got a job. I told God that if I got a job that I would minister to people. I received a phone call from a Pastor inviting me to become the next Pastor at the church where I am now. I returned to Gary in 1998.

What do you hope to leave as your legacy?

I hope to leave a legacy that will be a movement that goes on indefinitely and impacts people forever; however, I am still on a journey to define what that will be. My will is to live my life totally surrendered to what God wants to do with my life.

Chapter 7

A Life of Sports

The Life

of

Timothy Jones

In the words of

Coach Anthony Mabone

How did you meet Tim?

I met Tim on a football practice field at Horace Mann High School. I was the Defensive Coordinator at that time. Tim was working with the Offensive Coordinator and Head Coach. Tim and Coach Piggee had a disagreement so Coach Johnson agreed to help me work with Tim. At the time we had a D1 Prospect that Tim basically destroyed and all I could say was, "WOW." The guy outweighed Tim by 130 or 120 pounds. It was quite amazing to me, being that Tim had never played football.

What stood out about Tim as an Athlete?

Tim took on the D1 Prospect and made him look like he had never played before. I believed we had someone special. When we got into games Tim was even more remarkable, he was coachable and athletic. I began to learn where he came from and what he was dealing with in life. He was a young man in the streets, getting into trouble, doing whatever he wanted. I wanted to show him that football was a way to go to college, to see other parts of the country and understand that there is more outside of Gary. Even today, I coach to teach children about options in life.

The Journey of Coach Mabone

I attended Horace Mann High School and graduated in 1987. Then I attended Lakeland College in Cheboygan, Wisconsin and graduated in 1991. My college coach invited me to coach in Wisconsin, but Mr. Davis, the Assistant Principal at Horace Mann encouraged me to start coaching there in the summer of 1991. I coached at Horace Mann from 1991 until 2003. Then I coached at Tolleston Middle School 2003-2005, at the same time I was coaching at Lew Wallace High School. Then I went to coach at Thea Bowman Leadership Academy in 2007. I was the Head Coach for the first 3 years. Then I went to coach at Roosevelt 4 years and I returned to Thea Bowman for the last 3 years.

Coach Mabone, The Interrupter

Tim had an injury; however, he returned to the field to play football. We were practicing and a group of about six young men started coming toward the practice field at Horace Mann to fight Tim. He began to walk toward them, preparing to fight.

I made it very clear to them that if they stepped on the field they would not only have to fight Tim, but the whole football team. They returned to their cars and left that day. I never asked Tim about the situation after that day. I coach children to instill the reality that there is a better way of life.

The environment where I grew up had the same obstacles, but I decided to make different choices. I was never associated with a gang because I was clear about my dreams and the direction of my life. I made a choice to follow a different path because of my upbringing. I am a man cut from a different cloth. I knew early on that I wanted to go to college and play football. That is why I kept my focus. I wanted to play professionally, but my reward today is seeing children that I once coached who are now established and pursuing their dreams and goals. I have coached thousands of children in 24 years.

How did you find out about the incident when Tim was shot in the head?

Some of the other students considered Tim as a son to me. Therefore I was very hurt when I heard about the shooting. When I saw Tim with his brother David attending a football game at Horace Mann High School he was being pushed in a wheelchair. I was so hurt because that is the life that I was trying to keep Tim away from and I knew he was close to going to college. The opportunity to go to college would have led to greater opportunities for him. When I saw Tim at the game he had no memory, he was not talking, he was still going through therapy and he did not recognize me. It was so painful seeing Tim around friends that he was not able to recognize.

What are your hopes and dreams for Tim today?

Today I can say that Tim is definitely blessed. He is relentless. I hope that whatever he wants to do that he can still do it. When Tim told me that he had gotten saved and given his life to God I knew he was on the right track.

As a Coach, what is your source of strength to mentor young men?

As a Coach my source of strength is Jesus. I do everything through Christ who strengthens me. I coach to give back to my community; to teach children to associate the game of football with the game of life; to learn the importance of earning good grades and pursuing their dreams. I live the life I teach for the sake of the students that I coach.

What do you hope to leave as your legacy?

A lot of guys at work don't understand my life because I work shift work without a set schedule and I coach high school football. However, I am living to leave a great legacy. I hope to leave a legacy where people know that I love doing what I am doing, I am sincere and I gave my all.

The Life

of

Timothy Jones

In the words of

Coach Wayne Brumm

How do you describe Tim?

I call him King Tim. He is a gentle giant with an overflowing bubbly personality. Tim is a man full of love, a real optimist and an over comer. He has encountered a lot in his life; that which most people are only familiar with through movies. He is living it every day and with a great attitude. He has found the source of love which helps him to make every day a masterpiece.

When did you meet Tim?

I met Tim when he was 14 or 15. He was full of energy, but unsure of which direction to channel his energy. As a Coach, I was determined to steer that energy in the right direction. They were all great children, just seeking to find their own way.

As a Coach, what was your source of strength to mentor young men?

I was raised in the church and I always had a strong faith in God. I had a great upbringing, my mother ruled by an iron will and my father ruled by an iron rod so I was very clear of right from wrong. I am very clear on how blessed I am.

God leads me right all the time and when I follow that lead I go in the right direction. I do understand that sometimes not all of us have equal opportunities and we don't all start from the same point or have the same resources. Therefore, I appreciate the young men and young women who did not have the resources that I had while I was growing. I work hard to share and to mentor all the children I have the opportunity to coach.

Did you ever experience any challenges with Tim?

I told the basketball team to go to bed at 9 p.m. so that they would be well rested for their championship game the next day. However, a group of girls were able to persuade Tim and some of his teammates to sneak out and go to a pool party. They lost that game and it became a teachable moment. The lesson that Tim said he learned from the experience was, "Listen to your Coach." Tim recalled the experience as if it happened yesterday, "I had a good time at the pool party; however, it was not worth disappointing my Coach and my team. I know I have made mistakes in the past and everyone has made mistakes in their past. However, it is important to learn from your mistakes and always move forward."

What stood out about Tim as an Athlete?

His strength and explosiveness stood out to me. He had muscles; he could run fast and jump high. He was blessed with the ability to move naturally. He was a big, strong child for his age.

What was his greatest accomplishment on your team?

His greatest accomplishment was finishing the season with us, because I can be rather demanding. Every time we left town and went to a practice it was a learning experience. Some children were not necessarily used to my coaching style. After teaching some of the same lessons over and over again, my voice would become louder and more animated. I am a strong, Type A, white guy, with high expectations. Some children who were not raised with their father would shy away from that; however Tim kept coming back. As a Coach, I was demanding self discipline; the ability to follow instructions; accountability; following rules and being responsible.

How did you find out about the incident when Tim was shot in the head?

His Mother, Brenda called me. We had developed a strong relationship with his Mother who had a lot on her plate. In addition to taking Tim from one practice to another, she was also working and taking care of three other sons. To help her and make it work for Tim I would often pick him up and take him to practices.

When Brenda called, we went to the hospital as soon as possible. There were several questions in my mind. "How bad was it and was it fatal?" Once we got there and saw him I wondered, "What quality of life would Tim have?" Then I wondered, "Ok what now, what will this evolve into for his life? Is Tim going to make it through this?"

It was not pleasant then and it is not pleasant now. Tim is definitely a survivor. Especially when you look at his smile and his enthusiasm, given what has transpired in his life.

There are people who have been richly blessed, but can't smile the way Tim smiles on a daily basis. Sometimes some of the worst things that happen to you can end up being the best thing that happens to you. I was diagnosed with cancer 25 years ago. At that time it was the worst thing that happened to me, but in retrospect, it is the best thing that happened to me. After the diagnosis, I got my priorities straight and I got more focused.

Maybe Tim would prefer that this did not happen, but he has made the most of it. Tim has learned from the experience and he has grown from the experience.

Made in the USA
San Bernardino, CA
04 July 2017